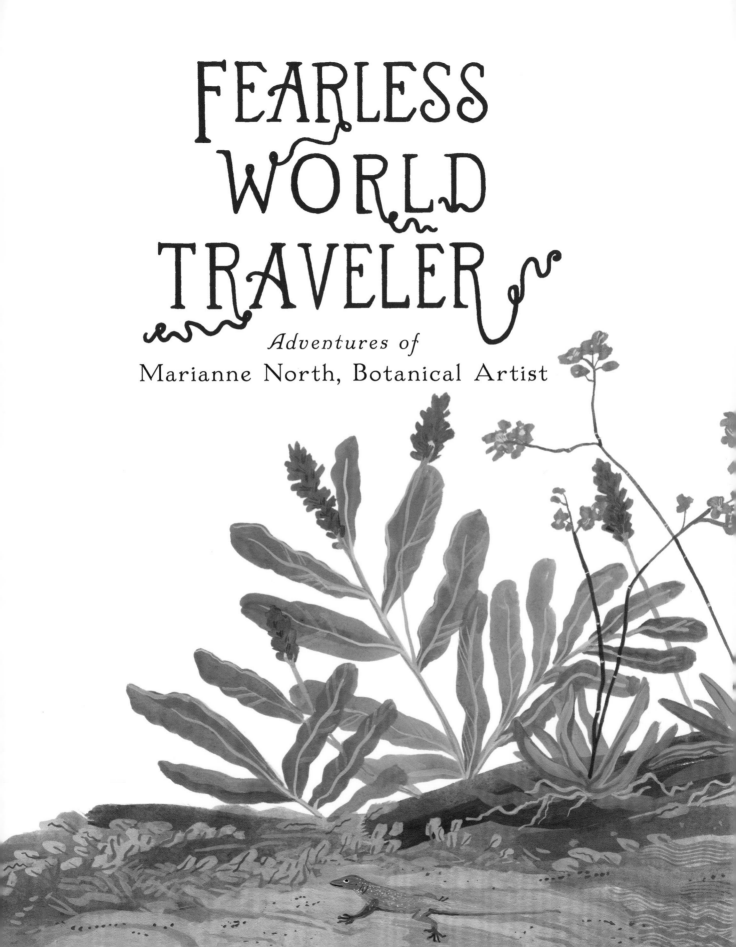

FEARLESS WORLD TRAVELER

Adventures of
Marianne North, Botanical Artist

by LAURIE LAWLOR

illustrated by BECCA STADTLANDER

HOLIDAY HOUSE · NEW YORK

When Marianne North was born on October 24, 1830, in her family's magnificent manor on the south coast of England, nobody thought she would amount to much.

By the time she was a teenager, she'd fallen head over heels in love with music. Sometimes she practiced singing and playing the piano eight hours a day. "Horrid noise!" her father complained. Art became her next fascination. Wherever she went, she carried a sketchbook to record her observations in pen and watercolor. Marianne's mother said she was wasting her time.

When Marianne discovered a passion for botany, her family laughed. Ridiculous! Marianne's father, a member of Parliament who owned three country estates and a house in London, refused to hire private tutors for her. Why bother? Women weren't allowed to vote, hold office, serve on juries, own property, sign contracts, earn college degrees, or become professional scientists.

Learn to behave like a proper young woman, everyone told Marianne, and one day, if you're lucky, you'll attract a rich husband.

Strong, tall, and restless, blue-eyed Marianne felt imprisoned in dismal drawing rooms. Tight corsets and stiff, floor-length gowns tormented her. Fancy balls in London were even more unbearable for shy Marianne. "A penance," she called them.

She decided to teach herself about plants. How? By reading books, studying nature, visiting botanical gardens and art museums, and asking questions of every art and plant expert she could find.

She began her quest when she was sixteen. Roaming alone in the fields and woods of her family's vast estate in northeast England, she hoped to find and paint every variety of fungus or mushroom listed in a thick, illustrated guide from a local library.

One day she rushed home with a mushroom the size of a turkey's egg. She tucked it beneath an overturned glass on her windowsill to watch it grow—just like a real scientist.

Pop! Crack! She awoke instantly the next morning. So did her family.

The mushroom had burst into an astonishing five-inch "stinkhorn" that shattered the glass and sprawled on the floor. Buzzing flies swarmed, attracted by the mushroom's rotten-meat odor. What a smell!

Marianne's family gave her the nickname "Pop."

Fortunately for Marianne, plenty of helpful, fascinating guests visited her parents' numerous homes. Her father's friends included famous astronomers, anthropologists, physicists, engineers, and botanists. Marianne enjoyed eavesdropping on the men's conversations and watching visiting landscape painters and botanical artists at work.

When an artist came to create a family portrait, she became enthralled by the bright colors of oil paints. She thought the paints would be perfect for flowers.

In 1855, Marianne's mother died. Although she was only twenty-four years old, Marianne promised that she would always take care of her irritable, demanding father. For the next fourteen years, she kept her word—supervising his household and serving as his travel companion. She never married.

When she suggested visiting the tropics to view plants her father balked. To please his disappointed "little Pop," he built her three heated greenhouses. Marianne still felt trapped and restless. Cold, damp winters triggered rheumatism so crippling, she had trouble holding a paintbrush.

When her sixty-nine-year-old father died in 1869 following a brief illness, Marianne was filled with grief and confusion. She was now forty. What next?

An elderly widow invited Marianne to go on a trip to North America in 1871. Marianne jumped at the chance to cross the Atlantic Ocean and quickly packed a large supply of tubes of oil paint, brushes, pens, and paper for the journey. The tour of the American East Coast and parts of Canada thrilled Marianne. Endless wilderness with so many new species entranced her. However, when her traveling companion's scolding became unbearable, Marianne went her own way.

She sailed to Jamaica to finally see the tropics. She didn't care that traveling alone was frowned upon for "unprotected ladies." From then on she would always travel by herself.

"Hurrah for liberty!" she wrote to a friend.

On Christmas Eve 1871, she stepped ashore in Jamaica and discovered a new world of balmy winds, fragrant blossoms, and lush trees swarming with shrieking birds. "I was in a state of ecstasy, and hardly knew what to paint first," she said.

She rented a run-down house in a secluded, wooded valley. Her workday started at sunrise, when she set off into the deep forest with paints, ink, paper, and easel. She painted without interruption—sometimes twelve hours a day.

After several months she returned to London with her finished paintings. Friends and family expected Pop to settle into a safe, ladylike life again. Marianne soon felt eager to escape. "I am a very wild bird," she told a friend. "I like my liberty."

Marianne gathered a few clothes and many art supplies and headed back to the tropics. She was no longer a traveler who painted. She had become a painter who traveled.

Between 1871 and 1885, Marianne trekked solo twice around the world, hunting for and painting rare and exotic plants on every continent except Antarctica. She visited fifteen countries—some more than once.

Travel wasn't easy. Journeys by steamship often took weeks. Typhoons and shipwrecks were constant dangers. To haul heavy art supplies, she used everything from local ox-drawn carts and lumber wagons pulled by mules to dugout canoes and sampans (small rowed boats with sails).

She spent long days in the saddle. When mountain paths turned too steep or mud-choked for horses, she hiked on foot. If bridges were washed out by flooding, she made long detours and dangerous crossings by log raft.

Without losing her balance she waded through water above her waist to cross streams in rain-soaked Brazilian jungles.

In Borneo she successfully shot rapids in a fragile canoe.

Swamp and jungle travel by canoe meant watching out for water snakes and alligators—not to mention ever-present leeches.

In India she rode evil-tempered camels and made journeys on the backs of elephants. "Like a walking tree and so slow!" she later said about the elephant rides.

Marianne slept anywhere—hammock, mat, or straw pallet. Often she shared her shelter with pesky rats, lizards, stinging ants, giant spiders, and poisonous snakes. More than once marauding crows tried to steal her glittering tubes of paint. Never a picky eater, she consumed anything—from squid to mangoes, from crabs to guavas. When food was scarce because of famine, she did not complain.

Travel exposed her to many tropical diseases, including dysentery, intestinal parasites, yellow fever, and malaria. No inoculations existed. She relied on local cures and her own hardy constitution.

Marianne often depended on the generosity and plant knowledge of native people. Although she found much to admire about how they lived in harmony with nature, her letters sometimes reflected the prejudices of her privileged upbringing.

An early conservation pioneer, Marianne wrote about the alarming devastation she encountered—clear-cut forests, rampant invasive species, and water pollution. She wasn't afraid to criticize the British Empire for plundering colonial resources, or American commercial loggers who seemed intent on cutting down every giant redwood in California.

Sadly, in many cases her paintings are the only remaining record of rare species that are now extinct.

As her collection of paintings crowded her London flat, Marianne began to wonder how she could share what she'd worked so hard to discover and illustrate. How could her artwork reach the most people—ordinary viewers and scientists alike?

While standing in a weary crowd on an English railway platform on August 11, 1879, she had a brilliant idea. In haste, she wrote a letter to her friend Sir Joseph Hooker, botanist and director of the Royal Botanic Gardens, Kew, offering to donate her entire collection of paintings and to pay for the design and construction of a special gallery in a quiet part of the gardens. To her delight, the Kew Gardens officials accepted. She hired an architect and began planning construction of the Marianne North Gallery.

While her gallery was under construction, she spent two years on an exhausting marathon journey exploring and painting in Australia, Tasmania, and New Zealand. She traveled by steamer to Hawaii and California, crossed the United States by train, and returned to England.

On June 7, 1882, the Marianne North Gallery opened to record crowds and acclaim from London newspaper reviewers. On display were 627 paintings, each described in a printed catalog. Before the invention of color photography or wildlife film documentaries, Marianne's vivid images of exotic plants, animals, and landscapes offered views few people had ever seen.

Visitors' enthusiasm, Marianne said, "gives me fresh courage to go on."

A few months later she left for South Africa, where she completed 110 paintings

in nine months. During the next two years, in spite of exhaustion, growing deafness, rheumatism, and other health problems, she made a five-thousand-mile trip to the Seychelles, islands off the coast of Africa. Next she made an arduous journey to South America. Her final quest? Painting the rare monkey puzzle tree in mountainous Chile.

When she finally arrived in London in 1885, she spent the next year rearranging and expanding the gallery, which now contained 848 paintings.

Marianne fled the hubbub of London two years later for a small, isolated cottage in the rolling countryside. She took along boxes of travel souvenirs—a stuffed Australian koala bear and platypus, shells, and crystals. As soon as she moved in, she ordered the tennis court torn out to make room for a garden.

Friends and relatives came to visit. Through the dark, cold winters, Marianne huddled near the fireplace and worked on the 1,727-page manuscript of her autobiography, *Recollections of a Happy Life*. To escape the chill (if only in her mind), she painted from memory palm-fringed beaches and azure water.

On August 30, 1890, fifty-nine-year-old Marianne died after a lingering illness. She was buried near her garden filled with the plants and flowers she loved so much.

Marianne North had never given up on her dream to do something remarkable that no one expected. Her determination, courage, and curiosity remained with her to the end.

"Did I not paint?" she wrote of her life. "And wander and wonder at everything?"

Marianne North's Legacy

PAINTINGS

Marianne North broke the rules. Self-taught and eager to experiment, she created paintings that crossed the boundaries between art and science. Unlike traditional botanical illustration of her time, which often showed, in pale watercolor, an individual plant specimen floating in space on a white background, Marianne's accurate work was done in brilliant oil paint, with the plant in the foreground and the landscape of its "home" in the background.

When she discovered a flower to paint, she sat still and observed shadows, colors, curves, and textures. Light, weather, and the fullness of blossoms changed by the minute. She worked in a race against time—ignoring rain, scorching temperatures, and biting mosquitoes. She wanted to capture surrounding plants and the landscape of her subject's environment. Using ink, she rapidly sketched details—including birds, insects, bats, lizards, and snakes that came to visit. She squirted paint directly from tubes onto paper and used a brush to re-create what she saw. When she ran out of paper, she used both sides.

Intrepid Marianne recorded a giant crimson carnivorous pitcher plant in Sarawak, Borneo, that no one in Europe had ever seen before. It was named *Nepenthes northiana* in her honor. Other plants named for her include *Northia seychellana*, a tree in the Seychelles; *Crinum northianum*, a kind of amaryllis; *Areca northiana*, a feather palm; and *Kniphofia northiana*, an African torch lily.

Not long after Kew Gardens accepted her donation, Marianne was honored by an invitation to show a few of her paintings to elderly, affable writer, scientist, and evolution pioneer Charles Darwin. "He was, in my eyes, the greatest man living," she wrote after visiting his home. Impressed by her work, he told her she must go to Australia, Tasmania, and New Zealand to complete her collection. She viewed this as "a royal command."

During fourteen years of intensive travel, Marianne resided in London a total of only three years. In an era before the invention of telephones or computers, her family and friends seldom knew her exact whereabouts. Handwritten letters took months to be delivered. Telegraph offices were located only in large cities, far from her remote destinations. Yet Marianne never stopped her solo painting journeys.

Since the opening of the Marianne North Gallery in 1882, her paintings have been almost continuously on display at Kew Gardens. This makes her exhibit one of the longest-running one-woman shows ever created. Today the gallery includes 832 of her paintings, arranged the way she wanted.

Walking into her splendid exhibit for the first time is like coming face-to-face with vibrant, blossoming chaos. All that's missing are the fragrance of vegetation, the calls of birds, and the buzz of insects. Grouped by geographic regions, the paintings of nearly a thousand species create a powerful mural effect because of the way they are displayed: from waist level to the ceiling, frame nearly touching frame. "Astonishing" is the best way to describe the visual impact.

An early visitor, who wandered in by accident while Marianne was still getting ready for the opening, was said to have been nearly knocked breathless by the display. When he was finally able to speak, he demanded, "It isn't true what they say about all these being painted by one woman, is it?" When Marianne replied that yes, she had indeed done them all, the man was flabbergasted. "You!" he declared. "Then it is lucky for you that you did not live two hundred years ago, or you would have been burnt for a witch." Marianne took this as a back-handed compliment.

In 2007, a team of professional conservators—specialists who repair and preserve works of art—started a two-year project cleaning and preserving the paintings, many of which were falling into disrepair from the effects of humidity. The team used scalpels to painstakingly remove backing boards from each painting. They cleaned the paintings with delicate swabs to remove dirt, and while looking through microscopes, used needles to reposition any tiny flecks of loose paint.

Like detectives, they were able to uncover hidden clues beneath the paint—Marianne's penciled notes and sketches. Ultraviolet light helped reveal chemical details about the paint she used. Microscopes uncovered tiny finds: clothing fibers, hair, seed cases, and pieces of insects—all of which may have accumulated as she worked in the field.

Thanks to a sizable grant from Britain's Heritage Lottery Fund and private donations, the Marianne North Gallery's restoration was completed in 2009. The roof and floors were replaced and new ventilation and lighting systems were installed in the Greek-temple-like structure.

Today the revitalized gallery remains open to the public and stands as a living testament to Marianne's energy and talent.

PUBLISHED WRITINGS

Marianne's autobiography, *Recollections of a Happy Life,* created from her letters, journal entries, and reminiscences, languished after she died. To be published, her editor had said, the manuscript needed to be cut by half.

Unfortunately, this job fell to Marianne's sister, Catherine, seven years younger than Marianne, and precisely the kind of person Marianne had not wanted to edit "her racy, flowing style." Catherine described how she went to work with a will on Marianne's reminiscences, "pruning out any unkind remarks upon relations (of which there are plenty)." Many of these comments had to do with Catherine's husband and other family members, including older brother Charles, who was born in 1828, and half sister, Janet, born in 1817.

In the end, *Recollections of a Happy Life, Being*

the Autobiography of Marianne North—domesticated and sanitized—sold four thousand copies when it was published in two volumes in 1892. The following year another volume, called *Further Recollections of a Happy Life,* appeared. All three books followed correct Victorian etiquette and featured Catherine's name on the cover: "Edited by her sister, Mrs. John Addington Symonds."

SOURCES

Amelia Edwards Archive, Somerville College, Oxford, www.some.ox.ac.uk/library-it/special-collections/special-collections.

Moon, Brenda E. "Marianne North's *Recollections of a Happy Life*: How They Came to Be Written and Published." *Journal of the Society for the Bibliography of Natural History* 8, no. 4 (May 1978): 497–505. www.euppublishing.com/doi/10.3366/jsbnh.1978.8.4.497.

———. Biographical note in *A Vision of Eden: Life and Work of Marianne North.* New York: Holt, Rinehart and Winston, 1980.

North, Marianne. *Recollections of a Happy Life, Being the Autobiography of Marianne North.* Edited by Mrs. John Addington Symonds. 2 vols. London: Macmillan, 1892.

———. *Further Recollections of a Happy Life.* 1 vol. London: Macmillan, 1893.

———. *Recollections of a Happy Life, Being the Autobiography of Marianne North.* Reprint of Volume 1, edited by Susan Morgan. Charlottesville: University Press of Virginia, 1993.

Ponsonby, Laura. *Marianne North at Kew Garden.* London: Webb and Bower, 1990.

SOURCE NOTES

p. 9 "Horrid noise." North (1892), Vol. 1, p. 13.

p. 9 "Marianne's mother . . . time." Amelia Edwards Archive no. 258, North letter, August 7, 1882.

p. 11 "a penance." Amelia Edwards Archive no. 245, North letter, July 19, 1871.

p. 14 "Pop." North (1993), p. 13.

p. 21 "Hurrah for liberty!" Amelia Edwards Archive, North letter, November 1871.

p. 23 "I was . . . first." North (1892), Vol. 1, p. 83.

p. 24 "I am . . . my liberty." Ponsonby, p. 19.

p. 30 "Like a walking tree and so slow!" Marianne North Papers, Letters to Dr. Coke Burnell, Royal Botanical Gardens, Kew Archive, April 30, 1878.

p. 36 "gives me . . . go on." Moon, *A Vision of Eden,* p. 34.

p. 40 "Did I not . . . everything?" North (1892), Vol. 1, p. 187.

p. 41 "He was, in my eyes, the greatest man living," (1892), Vol. 1, p. 87.

p. 41 "a royal command." North (1892), Vol. 1, p. 87.

p. 42 "It isn't true . . . a witch." Losano, Antonia, "A Preference for Vegetables: The Travel Writings and Botanical Art of Marianne North," *Women's Studies,* 1997, Vol. 26, p.430.

p. 42 "her racy, flowing style." Moon, "Marianne North's *Recollections,*" p. 503.

p. 42 "pruning out . . . plenty)." Ibid. p. 503.

WHO'S WHO

Some of the scientists, writers, politicians, and artists Marianne North encountered in her life and travels

Valentine Bartholomew, Queen Victoria's flower painter (1799–1879)

Dr. Arthur Burnell, Sanskrit scholar and botanist living in India; Marianne North collaborated, as illustrator, on his unfinished book about sacred plants (1840–1882)

Julia Margaret Cameron, photographer who met Marianne North in Ceylon in 1877 (1815–1879)

Charles Darwin, writer and scientist who wrote the path-breaking book on evolution, *On the Origin of Species* (1809–1882)

Robert Dowling, Australian oil painter (1827–1886)

Amelia Edwards, writer and Egyptologist (1831–1892)

Sir Frances Galton, anthropologist (1822–1911)

Sir Davies Gilbert, engineer (1767–1839)

Ulysses S. Grant, American Civil War general and President of the United States (1822–1885)

Sir Joseph Hooker, botanist and explorer who took over as director of the Royal Botanic Gardens, Kew, from his father, William Hooker (1817–1911)

Sir William Hooker, botanist and director of Kew Gardens (1785–1865)

William Holman Hunt, painter (1827–1910)

Edward Lear, landscape painter and poet who created "The Owl and the Pussycat" and other nonsense rhymes (1812–1888)

Henry Wadsworth Longfellow, American poet (1807–1882)

Sir Edward Sabine, astronomer and physicist (1788–1883)

PICTURE CREDITS

Reproductions of Marianne North's paintings appear on the endpapers. All of the images on the endpapers are copyrighted by and used with permission from Royal Botanic Gardens, Kew. Copyright © RBG KEW

On the left side:

Upper left: foliage, flowers, and fruit of the pitanga, also called the Suriname cherry, *Eugenia uniflora*, and sulphur butterflies. Jamaica.

Upper right: Two flowering shrubs, the brilliant red *Schotia speciosa* and the white Gardenia *thunbergia* and a type of trogon bird. Natal, South Africa.

Lower left: Wildflowers, the orange trumpet vine, *Bignonia venusta*, red morning glory, *Ipomoea nationis* (white flowers) and *Luhea rufescens*. Morro Velho, Brazil.

Lower right: Michelia tree, *Michelia excelsa*, and a vine, *Porana grandiflora*. Darjeeling, India.

On the right side:

Upper left: Papaw tree, *Carica Papaya*, with flowers and fruit. Central America.

Upper right: Dragon's Blood Tree, *Dracaena draco*. Tenerife, Canary Islands.

Lower left: Foliage, flowers, and fruit of a Queensland Tree, *Macadamia ternifolia*, and a red-tailed black cockatoo, *Calyptorhynchus banksia*. Queensland, Australia

Lower right: Tamarind tree, *Cojoba arborea*, and a type of barbet bird. Jamaica.

To my traveling companions,
Keira, Vivian, Beau, and Dean
—L.L.

For the wanderers, the curious, and the wild
—B.S.

Text copyright © 2021 by Laurie Lawlor • Illustrations copyright © 2021 by Becca Stadtlander
All Rights Reserved • HOLIDAY HOUSE is registered in the U.S. Patent and Trademark Office.
Printed and bound in January 2021 at C&C Offset, Shenzhen, China. • The artwork was created on watercolor paper
with black ink, watercolors, and colored pencil. • www.holidayhouse.com • 1 3 5 7 9 10 8 6 4 2

Library of Congress Cataloging-in-Publication Data
Names: Lawlor, Laurie, author. | Stadtlander, Becca, illustrator. | Title: Fearless world traveler : adventures of Marianne North,
botanical artist / by Laurie Lawlor ; illustrated by Becca Stadtlander. | Description: New York : Holiday House, [2021]
Includes bibliographical references. | Audience: Ages 6–9 | Audience: Grades 4–6 | Summary: "The vibrant and daring life of
Marianne North, a self-taught artist and scientist who subverted Victorian gender roles and advanced the field of botanical illustration"
—Provided by publisher. Identifiers: LCCN 2020040464
ISBN 9780823439591 (hardcover) | Subjects: LCSH: North, Marianne, 1830-1890—Juvenile literature.
Botanical artists—Great Britain—Biography—Juvenile literature.
Botanical illustration—Juvenile literature. Classification: LCC QK98.183.N67 L39 2021
DDC 581.941—dc23
LC record available at https://lccn.loc.gov/2020040464

ISBN: 978-0-8234-3959-1 (hardcover)